Merry Christmas 1989
To My Beloved Sister.

Mar.

THE NATURE NOTES
OF AN
EDWARDIAN LADY

The publisher has kept faithfully to Edith Holden's spelling,
punctuations and quotations throughout the text.

Text and illustrations copyright © 1989 by Rowena Stott

First U.S. Edition

Library of Congress Cataloging–in–Publication Data

Holden, Edith, 1871-1920.
The nature notes of an Edwardian lady / Edith Holden.
      p.   cm.
"Though published as the sequel to The country diary,
this journal of Holden's ... entitled by her simply,
Nature notes for 1905, is actually The country diary's
predecessor by a year."
ISBN: 1–55970–044–0
1. Natural history – England – Warwickshire.
2. County life – England – Warwickshire.
3. Illustrators – England – Biography.
I. Holden, Edith, 1871-1920.
Country diary of an Edwardian lady.
II. Title.
QH138.W37H65 1989
508.424'8 – dc20   89-6890 CIP

The publisher would like to thank Rowena Stott, Edith Holden's
great-niece and copyright holder of this work.
who has made the publication of this book possible.

The publisher would also like to thank Nancy White, custodian
of this diary for many years; her father-in-law, Ernest White,
who bought and cherished it before her, until his death in 1959;
and Susan White, who made faithful publication of this book possible.

Published in the United States by
Arcade Publishing, Inc., New York,
a Little, Brown company

Originally published in Great Britain by
Webb & Bower (Publishers) Limited
in association with Michael Joseph Limited

10 9 8 7 6 5 4 3 2 1

Designed by Peter Wrigley

PRINTED IN THE NETHERLANDS BY ROYAL SMEETS OFFSET BV, WEERT

1905

THE NATURE NOTES
OF AN
EDWARDIAN LADY

Edith Holden

ARCADE PUBLISHING · NEW YORK

LITTLE, BROWN AND COMPANY

E.B. HOLDEN

Woodside
Knowle
Warwickshire

Nature Notes

1905

"Nature never did betray . . .
The heart that loved her, tis her privilege
Through all the years of this our life to lead
From joy to joy; for she can so inform
The mind that is within us; so impress
With quietness and beauty; and so feed
With lofty thoughts, that neither evil tongues
Rash judgements, nor the sneers of selfish men
Nor greetings where no kindness is, nor all
The dreary intercourse of daily life,
Shall ere prevail against us; or disturb
Our cheerful faith, that all which we behold
Is full of blessings."

January

This month received its' name from the god Janus who had two faces looking in opposite directions, and Macrobius states that it was dedicated to him, because from its' situation, it might be considered to be retrospective to the past and prospective to the opening year.

Feast-days etc.
Jan. 1st.   New Year's Day
Jan. 6th.   Epiphany, Twelfth Day
Jan. 25.   Conversion of St. Paul.

Folk-lore.   *"Janiveer*
                        Freeze the pot upon the fire."

"If the grass do grow in Janiveer   *"A wet January*
  It grows the worse for it all the year."   *A wet spring."*

"The blackest month of the year,
Is the month of Janiveer."

"As the day lengthens, so the cold strengthens."

January

Ivy and Moss
gathered in January

"Welcome, wild North-easter!
        Shame it is to see
Odes to every zephyr;
        Ne'er a verse to thee.

Welcome, black North-easter!
        O'er the German foam;
O'er the Danish moorland
        From thy frozen home.

Sweep the golden reed-beds,
        Crisp the lazy dyke;
Hunger into madness
        Every plunging pike.

Through the black fir-forest
        Thunder harsh and dry,
Shattering down the snow-flakes
        Off the curdled sky."

C. KINGSLEY; –

ODE TO THE EAST WIND.

January

"*O* *Winter! Ruler of the inverted year*
Thy scattered hair with sleet like ashes filled
Thy breath congealed upon thy lips, thy cheeks
Fringed with a beard made white with other snows
Than those of age; thy forehead wrapped in clouds,
A leafless branch thy sceptre, and thy throne
A sliding car, indebted to no wheels;
But urged by storms along its' slippery way."

COWPER.

"*T*he *wintry hedge was black*
The green grass was not seen
The birds did rest
on the bare thorn's breast
Whose roots, beside the pathway track
Had bound their folds oer many a crack
Which the frost had made between."

SHELLEY

There are some birds which are purely winter visitors to these islands, arriving in the Autumn and leaving for more northern lands with the approach of spring. Such among the smaller birds are the Fieldfare, Redwing; Mountain finch, Snow-Bunting, Grosbeak and Grey Shrike. These birds never or rarely breed in Britain. The Field-fare and Redwing nest in the large birch and pine forests of Sweden and Norway. These countries as well as Iceland, Lapland and Russia are the summer home of the Snow-bunting and Mountain Finch, while the Gros-beak and Grey Shrike are also met with in North America. The two latter birds are very rare in England.

January

Birds of all kinds are to be seen going about in large flocks
in the winter months, traversing the fields in search of food.
Among the birds who thus congregate together are – Rooks,
Wild Pigeons, Plovers, Missel thrushes, Field-fares, Red-
wings, Starlings, Sparrows, Buntings, Larks, Finches of all
kinds Tits, and Golden-crested Wrens. The Tits and Gold-
crests may often be seen going about the larch trees in
company. The latter are much more common than is
generally supposed; but they frequent pine and fir woods
and seldom go near dwelling-houses. Though retiring in
their habits they will allow themselves to be approached
quite closely when busily employed running over the twigs
in their search for insects. Many animals change the colour
of their coats during the winter months, Hares, Foxes and
Squirrels lose the prevailing ruddy tint of their fur and
become much greyer in colour; thus harmonising with the
low tones of the winter landscape, while in the North of
Britain, the Ptarmigan and Mountain Hares become as
white as the snow that covers the hillside.

Golden-crested
Wrens.

Winter berries
Privet, Hips and Haws.

January

Most conspicious among Winter berries in the hedge-rows are the bright scarlet Holly berries with their glossy green foliage; then perhaps the Hawthorn berries and the Hips – such as are left of them by the birds; and when the Winter is a severe one; there are not many to be seen by the time January comes. The Ivy and the Privet berries – both Evergreens, are not such favorites with the birds, and are rarely touched by them until they are hard-pressed by hunger.

Even in January the hedges are not void of all blossom; before Christmas the catkins on the Hazel and Alder are fully formed; and if the season be a mild one the Hazel Catkins may be seen with the blossoms fully expanded; as well as the tiny red stars of the female blossoms, before January is over. The Yew is also found in blossom sometimes in this month; while in the gardens Prim-roses, Aconites, Snowdrops and Yellow Jasmine are often to be found.

"When winter winds are piercing chill,
    And through the hawthorn blows the gale,
With solemn feet I tread the hill
    That over-brows the lonely vale.

O'er the bare upland, and away
    Through the long reach of desert woods,
The embracing sunbeams chasteley play,
    And gladden these deep solitudes.

Where, twisted round the barren oak,
    The summer vine in beauty clung
And summer winds the stillness broke,
    The crystal icicle is hung.

Where from their frozen urns, mute springs
    Pour out the river's gradual tide,
Shrilly the skaters' iron rings,
    And voices fill the woodland side.

January

Alas! how changed from the fair scene
    When birds sang out their mellow lay,
And winds were soft and woods were green,
    And the song ceased not with the day.

But still wild music is abroad,
    Pale, desert woods! within your crowd;
And gathering winds, in hoarse accord,
    Amid the vocal reeds pipe loud.

Chill airs and wintry winds! my ear
    Has grown familiar with your song;
I hear it in the opening year, –
    I listen and it cheers me long.'

'WOODS IN WINTER'. LONGFELLOW.

17

February

"And lastly, came cold February, sitting
In an old waggon, for he could not ride
Drawne of two fishes, for the season fitting,
Which through the flood before did softly glide
And swim away; yet had he by his side
His plough and harness fit to till the ground,
And tools to prune the trees, before the pride
Of hasting Prime did make them burgein round."

SPENSER. "FAERIE QUEEN".

"Sweet is the lore which Nature brings;
Our meddling intellect
Mis-shapes the beauteous forms of things
We murder to dissect.
Enough of Science and of Art
Close up these barren leaves,
Come forth, and bring with you a heart
That watches and receives."

WORDSWORTH.

February

Blackbird

Alder
Catkins.

CELANDINE

"Pansies, lillies, king-cups, daisies;
Let them live upon their praises.
Long as theres' a sun that sets;
Prim-roses will have their glory.
Long as there are violets,
They will have a place in story;
There's a flower that shall be mine.
Tis' the little Celandine."

Ere a leaf is on a bush
In the time before the thrush
Has a thought about her nest,
Thou wilt come with half a call,
Spreading out their glossy breast
Like a careless Prodigal;
Telling tales about the sun,
When we've little warmth, or none."   WORDSWORTH.

SNOWDROP.

"Thou first-born of the year's delight
Pride of the dewy glade,
In vernal green, and virgin white
Thy vestal robes array'd."   KEBLE.

21

February

Folk-lore etc. The ancient name of Februarius was derived from the verb februare, to purify, or from Februa, the Roman festival of general expiation which was celebrated through the latter part of this month.

Chief days. – Candlemas Day, the 2nd of February, St Valentine's Day, the 14th and St Matthias, the 24th.

"February fill dyke,
Be it black or be it white,
But if it be white
Its' the better to like."

"All the months of the year, curse a fair Februeer."

"If February brings no rain,
Tis neither good for grass nor grain."

"If Candlemas Day be fair and bright,
Winter will have another flight."
But if Candlemas Day be clouds and rain,
Winter is gone and will not come again."

All Nature seems at work;
Slugs leave their lair.
The bees are stirring—
Birds are on the wing;
And Winter slumbering
In the open air
Wears on his face
A dream of Spring.

S.T. Coleridge.

Willow Catkins
Robin
White Crocus
Winter Aconite

Hazel Catkins
Snowdrops
Toad
Yellow Crocus.

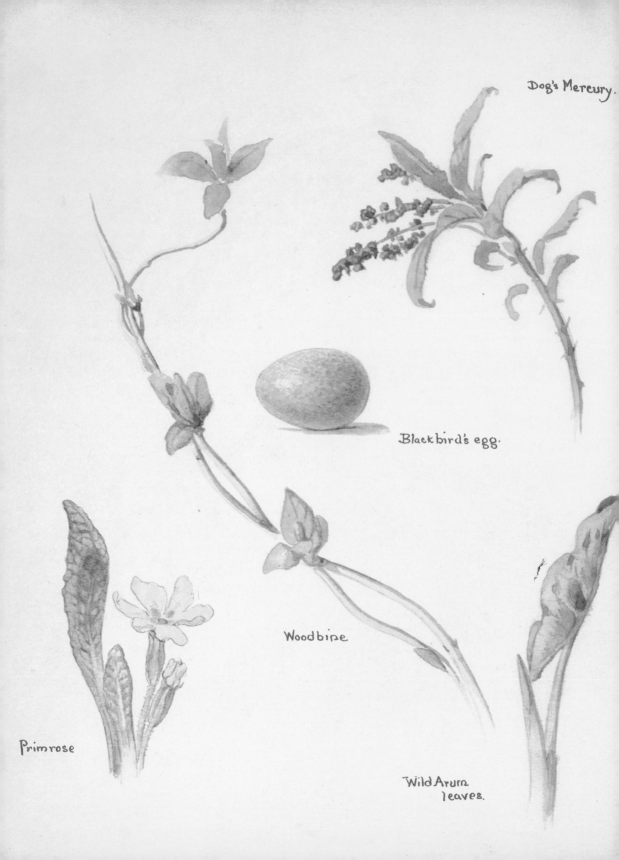

Dog's Mercury.

Blackbird's egg.

Woodbine

Primrose

Wild Arum
leaves.

Feb. 1st.   Saw the Dog's Mercury and Hazelnut in flower and the leaves of the Wild Arum opening.

3rd.   Found a black-bird's egg on the garden-lawn: Gathered willow-Catkins:

5th.   Picked up a dead Red-wing in the field. Snow-drops and Winter Aconites and primroses in blossom in the garden; also Crocuses.

9th.   Noticed the young nettle leaves coming up.

10th.   In the evening between 7 and 8 oclock saw the moon in the Western sky with Venus immediately below her and Jupiter a little above. Thrush, black-bird, robin, hedge-sparrow; and wren all singing this month. Honey-suckle foliage expanding; and green buds appearing on the Sycamore.

12th.   Heard the sky-lark singing. Gorse in blossom.

15th.   Found a queen Wasp crawling up the back of a chair.

17th.   Gathered Alder-catkins; green leaves unfolding on Elder.

19th.   Watched a pair of thrushes building their nest in the top of a high holly hedge in the garden. Partial eclipse of the moon visible, commencing 6. P.M.

20th.   Snow lying thickly on the ground.

23rd.   Elm-blossom and Birch Catkins in bud.

March

Folk-lore etc. The Romans called this month Martius from the God Mars; and it received the name Hlyd Monath, i.e. loud or stormy month from the Saxons.

Saints' Days etc. March 1st. St. Davids' Day.
March 12th. St. Gregory's. March 17th. St. Patrick's.
March 25th. Lady-Day.

"A peck of March dust is worth a king's ransom."

"March'll search ye, April try ye
May'll tell wether live or die ye."

"As many misties in March
So many frosties in May."

"March hack ham
Comes in like a lion
Goes out like a lamb."

"March borrowed from Averill
Three days and they were ill
The first it sall be wind and weet
The next it sall be snaw and sleet
The third, it sall be sie a frieze,
Sall gar the birds stick to the trees."

March

When rosy plumelets tuft the larch
And rarely pipes the mounted thrush;

Or underneath the barren bush
Flits by the sea-blue bird of March.

Tennyson.

March

"*It is the first mild day of March*
Each minute sweeter than before
The redbreast sings from the tall larch
That stands beside our door.

There is a blessing in the air,
Which seems a sense of joy to yield
To the bare trees, and mountains bare,
And grass in the green field."

WORDSWORTH.

Slayer of the winter, art thou here again?
O welcome, thou that bring'et the summer nigh!
The bitter wind makes not thy victory vain,
Nor will we mock thee for thy faint blue sky.
Welcome O March! Whose kindly days and dry
Make April ready for the throstle's song.
Thou first redresser of the winter's wrong!

WM. MORRIS.

"*The roaring moon of daffodil and crocus.*"

TENNYSON.

March

"*Daffodils that come before the swallow dares
And take the winds of March with beauty*".   SHAKESPEARE.

TO DAFFODILS

*Fair Daffodils, we weep to see
You haste away so soon;
As yet the early-rising sun
Has not attained his noon.
Stay, stay
Until the hasting day
Has run
But to the evensong;
And, having prayed together, we
Will go with you along
We have shoort time to stay, as you
We have as short a spring;
As quick a growth to meet decay
As you, or anything
We die
As your hours do, and dry
Away
Like to the summer's rain;
Or as the pearls of morning's dew,
Ne'er to be found again.*   ROBERT HERRICK.

Chaffinch. ♀♀♀
Hedge-Sparrow. ♀
Garden Daffodil

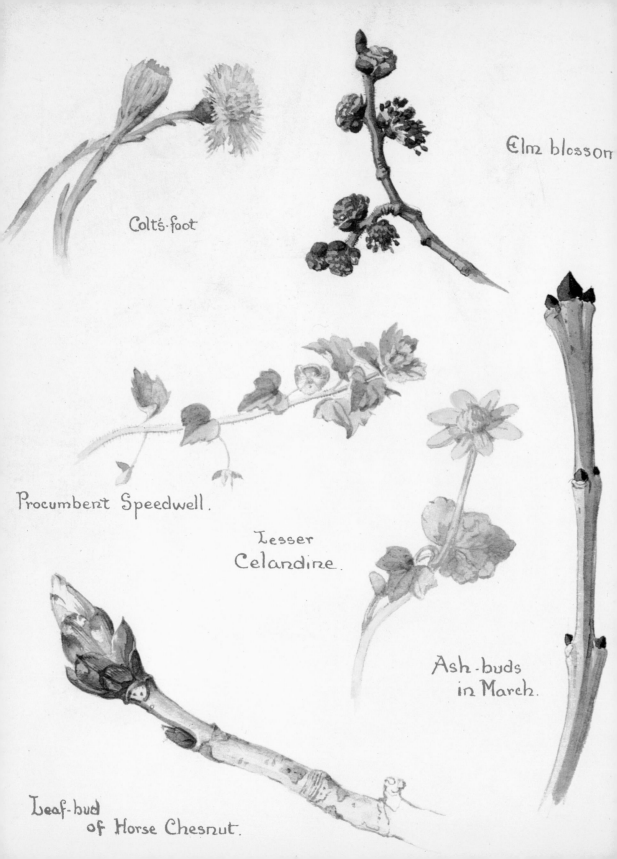

Colt's-foot

Elm blosson

Procumbent Speedwell.

Lesser
Celandine.

Ash-buds
in March.

Leaf-bud
of Horse Chesnut.

March 1st.   Dull, misty morning with cold showers of rain and sleet.

March 4th.   Beautiful, sunshiny afternoon, walked over to Hockly Heath and back by Lapworth & Packwood. On the way noticed the songs of the Thrush, Blackbird, Robin, Sky-lark, Hedge-sparrow, chaffinch and yellow-Hammer and the notes of the Tits. Whin-bushes in full bloom in many places. Coming home was struck by the colour of the cat-kins on the Alder trees, that glowed in fiery red masses in the rays of the setting sun.

March. 5th.   Green buds showing on the Hawthorn & Wild Rose.

March 8th.   Picked Colt's-foot and Procumbent Field Speedwell. Groundsel in flower and Chickweed. Rooks busy building their nests.

March 9th.   Saw a heron flying over the Blythe at Widney.

March 10th.   Pair of Blackbirds building their nest in the ivy against a wall. Strawberry-leaved Cinque-foil in bloom. Starlings building in the dove-cote.

March 15th.   Picked the Lesser Celandine. Yellow pollen showing on the Willow Catkins.

March. 19th.   Radiant Spring morning. Walked to Baddesley

Clinton by Tangle Lane, found quantities of prim-roses in blossom along the lane and on the sheltered banks of a pool. Sat on a felled beech trunk and watched the bees busy round the willow catkins, yellow with pollen; Noticed a great many hive-bees among them. Heard some turtle-doves cooing and watched a pair of mag-pies gathering sticks for their nest in the top of an oak-tree on the pool bank. Noticed the White Poplar trees in blossom.

March 21st. Two Thrushe's nests with eggs in the garden, in a laurel and an Arbor Vitae bush. Blackbirds' building in the holly hedge. Wrens building in the ivy against the house.

March 23rd. Watched a Robin building its' nest in the bank.

March 27th. Gathered three different species of Willow Cat-kins. Found a Robin's nest with three eggs in it; in the bank of a lane. Elm bushes coming into leaf and leaf buds of Horse-Chesnut opening.

March. 30th. Found a wren's nest built entirely of straw in the ivy growing up an ash-tree.

At the end of this month changed residence to Olton 5 miles further North.

APRIL

To Violets.

Welcome, maids of honour
You do bring
In the spring,
And wait upon her.

She has virgins many
Fresh and fair
Yet you are
More sweet than any

You're the maiden posies
And so graced
To be placed
'Fore damask roses.

Yet, though thus respected
By-and-by
Ye do lie,
Poor girls neglected.

Robert Herrick

Strawberry-leaved
Cinque-foil.

Wild
Straw-
-berry

Blackthorn
or Sloe in bud.

Wood
Sorrel.

Sand Martins.

Willow
Warbl[er]
or Willow Wre[n]

Bullace.

Chiff-chaff.

April

"The derivation of the name is unknown, though as far back as Varro we find the traditional etymology, - *'omnia aperit,* 'it opens every thing'; which is supported by comparison with the modern Greek use of the word 'opening' for Spring; while some would make out a connection with Aprodite, and Grimm suggests the name of a hypothetical God or hero, Aper or Aprus. Among the Romans this month was sacred to Venus.'

(ENCYCL. BRIT.)

Saints' Days etc.
23rd of April. St. George's Day. 24th. April St. Mark's Eve.

Folk-lore etc.

"April weather, rain & sunshine both together."

"When April blows his horn;
Tis good for both hay and corn."

"An April flood carries away the frog & his brood."

April

"When proud-pied April, dressed in all his trim;
Hath put a spirit of youth in everything."   SHAK. SONNET XIII.

"O, to be in England
Now that April's there,
And whoever wakes in England
Sees, some morning, unaware,
That the lowest boughs and the brushwood sheaf
Round the elm-tree bole are in tiny leaf
While the chaffinch sings on the orchard bough
In England – now!

And after April when May follows,
And the white-throat builds and all the swallows!
Hark, where my blossom'd pear-tree in the hedge
Leans to the field and scatters on the clover
Blossoms and dew-drops, at the bent spray's edge –
Thats' the wise thrush; he sings each song twice over,
Lest you should think he never could recapture
The first fine careless rapture!
And though the fields look rough with hoary dew,
All will be bright when noontide wakes anew.
The buttercups, the little children's flower
– Far brighter than this gaudy melon-flower."   R. B.

40

Hark! hark! the lark
At Heaven's gate sings
And Phœbus 'gins arise;
His steeds to water
At those springs;
On chaliced flowers
That lies.

While winking mary-buds begin
To ope their golden eyes
With everything that pretty bin
My lady sweet arise!

Sky-lark

Marsh Marigold or Ranunculous

Daffodils.

I wander'd lonely as a cloud
That floats on high o'er vales and hills.
When all at once I saw a crowd;
 A host, of golden daffodils;
Beside the lake, beneath the trees
 Fluttering and dancing in the breeze.

Continuous as the stars that shine
 And twinkle on the Milky Way,
They stretched in never-
 -ending line
 A long the margin of a bay
Ten thousand saw I at a glance
 Tossing their heads in
 sprightly dance.

The waves beside them danced, but they
Outdid the sparkling waves
 in glee:
 A poet could not but be
 gay,
In such a jocund company:
 I gazed - and gazed -
 but little thought
What wealth the show to me
 had brought.

For oft when on my couch I lie
In vacant or in pensive mood,
 They flash upon that inward eye
 Which is the bliss of solitude.
 And then my heart with pleasure fills
 And dances with the daffodils.

                    W. Wordsworth.

Wild Daffodils

April

April. 1.   Still, warm, cloudy day. Gathered some wild Daffodils in a field.

April 3rd.   Saw two Sand-martins catching flies over Olton Mill-pool; saw the first Willow Warbler. Found a Black-bird's nest with one egg in it in some brambles; and another with three eggs, in a whin-bush.

April 4th.   Picked a spray of Blackthorn in bud.

April 5th.   Saw blossoms on the Wild Cherry and Larch, Found some Lesser Stitchwort in flower. Maple bushes in leaf also crab-apple, Larch, Wild cherry and Hazel; Watched a Hare and some Pheasants feeding in a Ploughed field.

April 7th.   Cold and stormy. Snow showers in the morning.

April 9th.   Gathered some sprays of Bullace in blossom.

April 11th.   Warm, close day with steady rain falling, went for a walk in the after-noon and discovered a marsh full of Ranun-culous in blossom. Found two Hedge-sparrows nests, one in a whin-bush with two young birds newly hatched and one egg in it, the other in a hawthorn hedge; picked some wild Anemones and Wood-sorrel and Ground Ivy. Saw a pair of Chiff-chaffs and some House-Martins.

April

"*T*he cowslips tall her pensioners be;
In their gold coats spots you see;
Those be rubies, fairy favours,
In those freckles live their saviours.
I must go seek some dew-drops here,
And hang a pearl in every cowslip's ear."

'MIDSUMMER-NIGHT'S DREAM'.

"*W*hen daisies pied and violets blue
And Lady's smocks all silver-white
And cuckoo buds of yellow hue
Do paint the meadows with delight.

SHAKESPEARE. – SONG.

"*T*he copse's pride, Anemones;
With rays like golden studs on ivory laid
Most delicate! But touched
With purple clouds;
Fit crown for April's fair but changeful brow."

"*C*an trouble live with April days,
Or sadness with the summer moons?"

TENNYSON

Ox-slip

Cuckoo-flower
or
Ladie's Smock.
Cow-slip.

Wild Cherry

Spring Vetch.

Wood
Anemone
or
Wind flowe

April

April 17th.   Made an expedition in search of wild flowers.
Went by train to Lapworth, walked across to
Bushwood, from there to Baddesley Clinton and then to
Knowle station and home by train. Flowers gathered –
Primroses Cowslips, Ox-slips, Cuckoo-flowers,
Strawberry Anemones, Early purple Vetch; White
Violets, Dog Violets, Wood-sorrel, Moschatel, Lady's
Mantle, Blackthorn, Bullace, Corn Crowfoot and
Common Lesser Sedge and Daisies. Bushwood was
carpeted with prim-roses and Anemones in places, and
I found a great number of Ox-slips growing among the
Cowslips on the banks and under the hedges in fields,
There was no trace of any blossoms of the Sweet Purple
Violet, though beds of their large heart-shaped leaves; I
found a number of White ones, so conclude they flower
a little later than the purple. The wild Pear was just
ready to break into blossom and the buds of Hawthorn
were very large.

April 17th   Coming along the canal, the towing-path was lined by the Lesser Sedge with its spikes of blue green leaves and spear-like blossoms just shooting up between them. Later the latter are very dusky in colour but just now they are wonderfully irridescent like the colours on a pigeon's neck. Saw a number of Chimney Swallows and House-Martins catching flies over the Canal. Saw great numbers of Chiff-Chaffs and Willow Wrens on the way to Bushwood. I noticed that many of the Ox-slips had single stems to each separate blossom like prim-roses. On one root all the flowers were on separate stalks to the root and looked like small Prim-roses, only deeper yellow and with the orange-star. Can this be caused by bee-fertilization? Saw a Sea-gull flying over-head quite low down; it had evidently been attracted by the reservoirs adjoining the canal at Kingswood.

House
Martins

Swallows.

Common Lesser Sedge.

Willow Wren's
egg

Willow Wren
and nest.

Hedge Sparrow's
egg

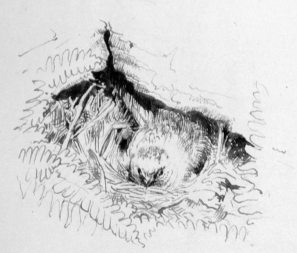

Robin and nest

Robin's egg

April

April 19th: Treacle Mustard in blossom.

April 24th.   Walked across Olton golf-course to Olton mill-pool;
The hawthorn hedges are quite green and some of the Sycamore
trees in full leaf. Gathered some of the blossom of the latter, also
of the Ash and some pink buds of Crab-apple. A Water-hen on
Olton Mill-pool was sitting on her nest in the middle of a bed of
reeds. She had built up her nest about two feet above the level of
the water, and looked as if she were perched up on a little
floating island.

April 28th.   Travelled down to Dousland on Dartmoor, through
Worcester, Gloucester, Bristol, and Exeter. Below Cheltenham
the oak-trees were in their first foliage of golden green, Fields
thick with Daisies and Cowslips, and coming through Somerset
and Devon the Red Campions and Wild Hyacinths were in
blossom on the banks.

April 28th.　　In the neighbourhood of Dawlish noticed quantities of White Sea-Campion and yellow Wall-flower covering the cliffs with patches of white and yellow. Rising up from Plymouth noticed how much more backward the foliage was on the high levels of Dartmoor.

April 29th.　　Wet, windy weather; Went through a little beech-wood where the foliage was breaking like a green mist among the grey stems; onto Yannadon Common, The Gorse is just in its' glory and will be for another month yet, The scent from the Gorse and the sweet soft air were most invigorating, Many Skylarks singing aloft in spite of the wind. Saw a Hawk poised over the eastern side of the down. Gathered some Whinberry blossom; A few shaggy little Dartmoor ponies were cropping the gorse on the down; one, with a wee brown foal by its' side.

　　The walls and banks here are a perfect mosaic of colour, with the fresh green of the young ferns, — English Maiden-hair and many other varieties, and Wild Strawberry, Dog Violet, Wild Geranium and other tiny flowers.

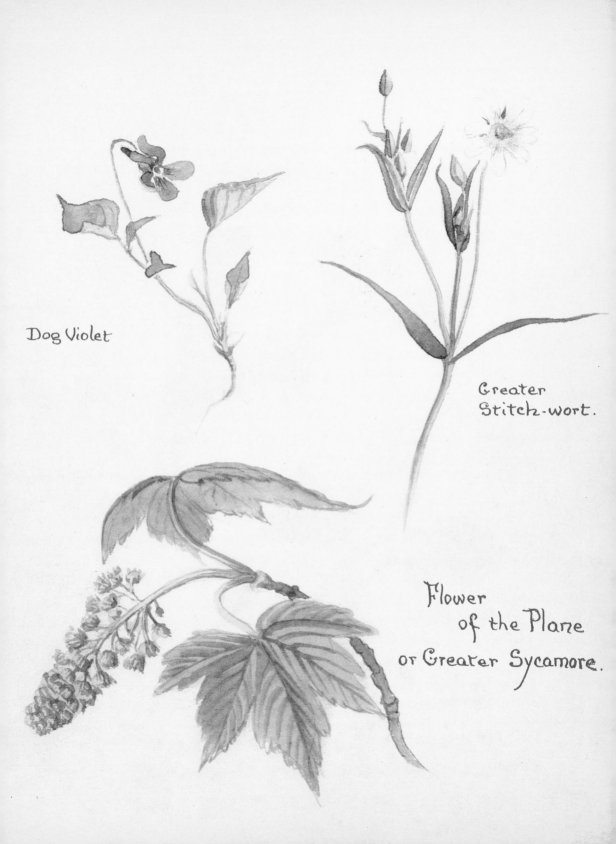

Dog Violet

Greater
Stitch-wort.

Flower
of the Plane
or Greater Sycamore.

Flower
of the
Ash.

Whin-berry

April

April 29th.   Gathered some Wild Geranium and Wild Hyacinth. Saw a lovely little Hedge-sparrow's nest in a Whin-bush with four eggs in it. The Gorse was in full bloom and made a glowing contrast with the blue eggs in the mossy nest.

April 30th.   Wild, stormy day of wind and rain.

*"H*ark! How the cheerful birds do chaunt their lays
And carol of Love's praise.
The merry lark his matins sings aloft
The Thrush replies, the Mavis descant plays,
The Ouzell shrills, the Ruddock warbles soft;
So goodly all agree with sweet consent
To this day's merriment."

E. SPENSER. 'EPITHALAMION'.

AN APRIL DAY

"When the warm sun that brings
    Seed-time and harvest, has returned again,
Tis sweet to visit the still wood where springs
    The first flower of the plain.

I love the season well
    When forest glades are teeming with bright forms
Nor dark and many-folded clouds foretell
    The coming on of storms.

From the earths' loosened mould
    The sapling draws its' sustenance and thrives
Though stricken to the heart with winter's cold
    The drooping tree revives.

The softly warbled song
    Comes from the pleasant woods, and coloured wings
Glance quick in the bright sun that moves along
    The forest openings.

When the bright sunset fills
    The silver woods with light, the green slope throws
Its' shadow on the hollows of the hills
    And wide the upland glows.

And when the eve is born
    In the blue lake the sky, o'er-reaching far
Is hollowed out, and the moon dips her horn
    And twinkles many a star.

Sweet April! – Many a thought
    is wedded unto thee, as hearts are wed
Nor shall they fail, till to its' Autumn brought
    Life's golden fruit is shed."

H. W. LONGFELLOW

Nature Notes

Dousland, Dartmoor, Devon.

"*It may indeed be only phantasy*
That I essay to draw from all created things
Deep, heartfelt, inward joy that closely clings
And find in leaves and flowers that round me lie
Lessons of love and earnest piety.
So let it be, — and though the whole world rings
In mock of this belief; to me it brings
Nor fear, nor grief, nor vain perplexity.
So will I rear my alter in the fields
And the blue sky my fretted dome shall be;
And the sweet fragrance that the wild flower yields
Shall be the incense that I offer thee -
Thee, only God, & Thou will not despise
Even me, the priest, of this poor sacrifice."

S. T. COLERIDGE

May

The name of this month is of doubtful origin. Ovid suggests Maia, the mother of Mercury, to whom the Romans were accustomed to sacrifice on the first day of the month. In the Roman Catholic Church May is known as "the month of Mary". May-day is the name given to the first day of the month in England, when in olden days the people went out at early dawn "a-Maying" to welcome the advent of spring.

Folk-lore etc.

> *"Change not a clout, till May be out."*

> *"Who doffs his coat on a winter's day*
> *Will gladly put it on in May."*

> *"Shear your sheep in May, & shear them all away".*

> *"A cold May and a windy, a full barn will find ye."*

> *"Be it weal or be it woe, beans blow before May doth go".*

"*Now rings the woodland loud & long*　　*And drowned in yonder living blue*
The distance takes a lovelier hue　　　*The lark becomes a sightless son*

TENNYSON.

58

May

Wild Geranium
or
Herb Robert.

Pink Campion.

May

Now the bright Morning star, day's harbinger,
Comes dancing from the East, and brings with her
The flowery May; who from her green lap throws
The yellow Cowslip and the pale prim-rose
Hail! flowery May that dost inspire
Mirth and youth and warm desire.
Woods and groves are of thy dressing
Hill and dale doth boast thy blessing
Thus we salute thee with our early song
And welcome thee and wish thee long.

MILTON. – MAY SONG.

"The year's at the spring,
The day's at the morn;
The morning's at seven;
The hillsides' dew-pearled;
The larks' on the wing;
The snails' on the thorn,
Gods' in his heaven;
Alls' right with the world."

R. BROWNING.

May

"The midges dance aboon the burn
The dews begin to fa'.
The pairtricks doon the rushy holm
Set up their evenin' ca'.
While loud and clear the blackbirds' sang
Rings thro' the briery shaw
And flittin' gay the swallows play
Around the castle wa'.

Beneath the golden, gloamin' sky
The mavis mends her lay;
The redbreast pours his sweetest notes
To charm the lingerin' day.
While weary yeldrins seem to wail
Their little nestlins' torn;
The merry wren fro' glen to glen
Gaes jinkin thro' the thorn.

The roses fauld their silken leaves
The foxglove shuts its' bell
The honeysuckle and the birk
Spread fragrance thro' the dell
Let others crowd the giddy court
Of mirth and revelry
The simple joys that Nature yields
Are sweeter far to me."

ROBERT TANNAHILL.

Sparrowhawk
and
Stoat.

Stone-chats.

Wheat-ear

May

May 1st.   Very windy, but bright sunshine. Walked to
Yelverton and sat on the moor, Watched a handsome little black-
headed Stone-chat 'jinkin' thro' the gorse; Follow'd him to
another patch of furse and sat down to watch. He scolded
terribly and presently the hen-bird came with a beakful of small
caterpillars and began to scold too. I moved my station and sat
down behind a big whin bush a few yards farther away;
but the hen-bird followed after swallowing her collection of
grubs and scolded and chattered at me for half an hour. At
last she flew away but soon returned with another beakful of
caterpillars, I kept very quiet and at last had my reward. The
mother bird suddenly dived down to the foot of a small gorse
bush a few yards away and came up with her beak empty.
I followed and discovered a cosy nest hidden away very
carefully among the dry grass at the roots of the gorse with five
baby stone-chats in it, nearly fledged.

May 1st.   I saw a great variety of birds on the moor, Meadow-pipits, Sky-larks, Buntings, Linnets and a beautiful Wheat-ear.

May 2nd.   Gathered Early Purple Orchis, Lesser Stitchwort, and Water Crowfoot; found two Blackbirds' nests with eggs.

May 3rd.   Two Chaffinchs' nests, Thrushe's nest and two Robins' nests. Golden Saxifrage in flower.

May 4th.   Walked to Burrator lake and down the glen beside the Meavy. Made a sketch of the still leafless oak-woods rising up on each side the combe, with Sheep's Tor just topping them.

Yellow Pimpernel in blossom among the rocks beside the river, and quantities of prim-roses and Wood-sorrel, The Wood-sorrel blossoms are wonderfully large here; Golden glory of Whins everywhere; On the road beside the lake, noticed a pair of Linnets collecting moss and feathers, watched them till they flew off to a patch of gorse bushes a little way up the hill-side.

Yellow Brimstone
Butterfly

Small Cabbage
Butterfly.

Purple Orchis   Marsh Violet

Blue
Pink
and
White
Milkwort

Lesser Speedwe
Tormentil.

May

May 4th.   The cock-bird kept sentinel on the top of a dead furse; After a short time they flew away and I soon discovered the nest in the thickest part of a whin-bush. Picked some London Pride on the walls. Saw a green Wood-pecker on the bank of the railway cutting, – looking for ants' nests I expect, and heard the Cuckoo for the first time this year. Found a ripe Strawberry.

May 5th.   Walked past Lowry to make a sketch of an old bridge over the Meavy. Brilliantly hot day, saw two Small Cabbage Butterflies and one Brimstone, going down Lowry Hill; Picked some Tormentil and blue Milkwort and Louse-wort off the banks and found some Marsh Violets in a bog; A Water Ouzel was bobbing about among the stones in the river where I was sketching and a Kestrel swooped past me and alighted in a field close by. Wonderful stretches of gorse blossom all round the shores of Burrator lake. Bulbous Buttercup in blossom. Saw a Stoat; and Trout in the Meavy.

May 6th.   Walked to Lowry quarry and round Burrator Lake. A Pied Wagtail's nest in a heap of cut granite in the quarry and a Black-bird's nest in a cleft in the rock. Pink Campion and common Bugle in flower.

May 8th.   Saw a little grey Lizard come out of a hole in a wall, he didn't seem frightened but sat on a stone blinking his eyes at me and basking in the sunshine. The bogs here are full of small white Water-Crowfoot; but I have seen no signs of Bog-bean, nor Butterwort nor Sundews, such as you find in the Welsh and Scotch marshes.

May 12th.   Eighth day without rain, and sixth of bright sunshine. I took my paint-box and a canvas and went to make a sketch of Leather Tor and the moor with the ponies. The high banks on each side the steep lane down to Lowry are covered now with small flowers; – Violets, Strawberry-flowers, Tormentil, Bilberry, and today I noticed for the first time the bright blue flowers of the Lesser Speedwell and blue and pink Milkwort.

Wild Hyacinths
&
Hedge-sparrow's nest

Small Copper Butterfly

Slow-worm
or
Blindworm

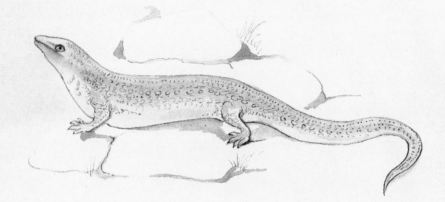

Lizard

Yellow-Trout.

May

May 12th   A Blindworm crept out from some dead grass at the foot
of a wall within a yard of where I was sketching, it was about a
foot long. It wriggled round the roots of a thorn bush and then
crept half its' length under some dead bracken; leaving its tail in
the sunshine. When I touched it, it didn't move and remained
quite passive even when I moved it about with a stick.

    Had an endless tramp over the bog after the ponies; there
were about half a dozen of them feeding among the gorse on the
moor sloping down to Burrator lake. They were all different
colours, from black to light chestnut. One tiny mouse-coloured
foal about a week old, kept running in circles round and round
its' mother and skipping in the air like a lamb. I walked right
down to the shore of the lake, the little glades in between the
boulders were blue with wild Hyacinths. I found a quantity of
Sundews in the bog for the first time here.

May

May 12th. On the way home I found a Linnets' nest with one egg in it in a whin-bush just below the quarry, and immediately below a Robin was sitting on its' nest in the bank. Saw a Small Copper Butterfly and a Small Tortoise-shell; and the caterpillars of the latter butterfly.

May 13th. Went to the top of Sheep's Tor.

May 14th. Saw a little yellow Lizard on a bank; I thought I would capture it and bring it home to sketch, but it slipped through my fingers and when I caught it by the tail, to my horror it snapped itself free, leaving the end of its' tail wriggling in my fingers!

May 18th. Went through Walkhampton to Huckworthy Bridge. The ferns along the river-side were very luxuriant, all kinds – Harts' Tongue; Male, Lady, Hard, English Maiden-hair, Shield and many others whose names I did not know. A little hawthorn tree among the boulders was just coming into blossom; they are scarce in this part.

Hawthorn blossom.
Small Tortoise-shell Butterfly

Buttercup
Yellow Pimpernel.

Ivy-leaved Toadflax.

Wood Sanicle.
Orange-tip Butterflies.

Field Scorpion Grass
Evergreen Alkanet

Ladie's Fingers and Thumbs
Wall Butterfly

Hawkbit

May

May 18th.   In a meadow by the river I picked a great many flowers.
– Blue Borage; Monkey-flower (Mimulus); Campion; Blue-bells,
Prim-roses; Buttercups; Purple Vetch, Purple Orchis,
Stitchwort, yellow Pimpernel, Wild Geranium and a kind of Wild
For-get-me-not. Picked some Ivy-leaved Toadflax from a wall on
the way home; and saw an Orange-tipped Butterfly; Meadow
Browns and White Butterflies, Large and Small, have been
plentiful the past few days.

May 20th.   Gathered Pink Clover and Black Meddick; Saw a dead
Slow-worm in the road.

May 25   Went to the top of Peak Hill, gathered Samphire in a
plantation on the Prince-town road, Ladies fingers and thumbs
and a kind of small Hawkweed in blossom on the banks. Saw a
Peacock Butterfly and picked some Brooklime.

May 28th.   Went to Lowry to sketch, In the bog by the lake-side
gathered small Water For-get-me-not, Cotton Grass, Lesser
Spearwort and Sundew. Saw the broken shells of some
Pheasant's eggs on the moor coming home.

May 29th   Saw a Painted Lady Butterfly, gathered some Greater Celandine and Large Hawk-weed. Quantities of deep crimson Campions in flower among the Hyacinths.

This month has been one of the dryest Mays I ever remember. We have only had one wet day and one or two showers during the whole of it.

SUMMER

What was Summer chanting?
*   "Oye brooks and birds,*
Flash and pipe in happiness
Stirring hearts that cares oppress
*   Into shining words!*
Here's a maze of butterflies
Dancing over golden gorse
Here's a host of grassy spies
Sunshine has set free, of course!
Wonder at the wind that blows
Odours from the forest sweet;
Marvel at the honeyed rose
Heaping petals at her feet,

Hark at wood nymphs rustling thro'
Brakes and thickets tender-knee'd!
Hark! Some shepherd pipe there blew!
Was it Pan upon a reed?
Oh, the pinks and garden-spice
Natures' every fair device,
Mingled in a scented hoard
Expected; longed-for,
and adored –
Summer's come!"

NORMAN GALE.

Small Water For-get-me-not   Lesser Spearwort   Cotton Grass

Pea-cock Butterfly

Silver-weed
Creeping Cinquefoil
Thyme-leaved Speedwel

June

Ovid assigns the name of this month to Juno; others connect it with the Consulate of Junius Brutus. The principal days observed in this month are

June 11th.   St Barnabas
June 24th.   Midsummer Day
June 29.   St. Peter

"Mist in May and heat in June
Brings all things into tune."

"A dripping June keeps all in tune."

"June damp and warm does the farmer no harm."

"Barnaby bright, (June 11th) all day and no night."

"St Barnabas, mow your first grass."

June

O June, O June, that we desired so,
Wilt thou not make us happy on this day?
Across the river thy soft breezes blow
Sweet with the scent of bean-fields far away
Above our heads rustle the aspens grey.
Calm is the sky with harmless clouds beset.
No thought of storm the morning vexes yet."

WM. MORRIS – EARTHLY PARADISE.

"Roses and honeysuckle melting into the blue,
Green bowers overhanging; tall grass drenched
          with dew.
Small birds, twittering; warbling,
Hidden in the shade.
Sweetest fragrance wafted;
From every hedge and glade.
All as full of sweetness and song
As it can hold;
June in all her beauty of blossoms manifold.

June

Yellow Iris
Dragon-fly
Mare's Tail.

To the Cuckoo.

O blithe new-comer! I have heard,
I hear thee and rejoice:
O Cuckoo! Shall I call thee Bird?
Or but a wandering Voice?

While I am lying on the grass
Thy twofold shout I hear;
From hill to hill it seems to pass,
At once far off and near.

Though babbling only to the vale
Of sunshine and of flowers
Thou bringest unto me a tale
Of visionary hours.

Thrice welcome darling of the Spring
Even yet thou art to me.
No bird, but an invisible thing.
a voice, a mystery

The same whom in my school-boy days
I listened to, that cry
Which made me look a thousand ways
In bush, and tree, and sky.

To seek thee did I often rove.
Through woods and on the green;
And thou wert still a hope, a love.
Still long'd for, never seen.

And I can listen to thee yet
Can lie upon the plain
And listen, till I do beg
That golden time again

O blessed Bird! the earth we p[...]
Again appears to be
An unsubstantial faery plac[...]
That is fit home for thee.

W. Wordsworth

June

June 1st.   Fine, bright day.

June 2nd.   Went down to a little stream, running into the Walkham. Found a great bed of Yellow Irises in blossom and among them a very large species of Mimulus with yellow and orange flowers.

June 3rd.   Stormy day, mist blotting out all the moors.
          Gathered Silver-weed and Water-cress in blossom, and a small species of St. John's wort, and a pretty little purple speedwell which is coming out on the walls this month.

June 4th.   Picked Yellow-Rattle, Pink and Scarlet Clover and saw some Moon Daisies in a field. Gathered Foxgloves.

June 7th.   Walked to the old bridge over the Meavy past Lowry, visited the bog where the Marsh Violets grow, there were plenty of leaves but no flowers left; The bog was full of tall pink Marsh Louse-wort and Cotton-grass, and quite blue in some places with small Water Forget-me-not; I also gathered the Spotted Orchis and Eye-bright, and Burnett in bud.

June

Two young fair lovers
Where the warm June wind
Fresh from the summer fields
Plays fondly round them
Stand tranced in joy.

With sweet, joined voices,
And with eyes brimming;
'Ah' they cry 'Destiny,
Prolong the present!
Time, stand still here!'

So, some tempestuous morn in early June
When the year's primal burst of bloom is o'er.
Before the roses and the longest day –
When garden-walks and all the grassy floor
With blossoms red and white of fallen May
And chestnut flowers are strewn –
So have I heard the cuckoo's parting cry,
From the wet field, through the vex't garden-trees;
Come with the volleying rain and tossing breeze:
The bloom is gone, and with the bloom go I!

MATTHEW ARNOLD. "THYRSIS."

88

Yellow Rattle

Moon Daisies
Pink and White Clover

" I saw a foxglove one soft summer's e'en;
That rose erect and tall in leafy gloom;
It's lifted finger mid the woodland scene,
A crimson spire of everdwindling bloom

In sooth, I ne'er beheld a form more fair,
To challenge thought and counsel simple joy
To conjure draughts of that diviner air
Whose subtle sense our follies still destroy

I could not count the long-lipped bells
that hung
With spotted throats each close on
each at rest,
As mounting still the tapering wand,
they clung,
And left unfaltering unity expressed."

E.M.H.

"The foxglove tall
Sheds it's loose purple bells
or in the gust,
Or when it bends beneath
the upspringing lark,
Or mountain-finch alighting

S.T. Coleridge

Fox·gloves
&
Male Fern .

June 7th.   On the way home I stopped to look in the linnets' nest at
Lowry, the four baby birds were nearly fully fledged; such a
nestful of soft, downy brown feathers they made. I also found a
Wren's nest of dead bracken hung among the brambles by the
river-side, I pushed down the little door-way with my finger to
look in; one of the parent-birds was at home, sitting close but she
never stirred from her place. Another wren's nest of moss
hanging from the wall above a spring was full of baby birds:

June 9th.   Gathered some Deadly Night-shade down by the
Iris-beds; also Bladder Campion and Wall Pennywort. Saw
a Painted Lady and a Small Blue Butterfly. Rowan-tree in
blossom and Elder-tree.

June 15th.   Went to Lowry Crossing to sketch pony and foal.
The grass in the field was full of tiny flowers, a tiny species of
Madder – with pale lilac flowers; a small purple Geranium,
scarlet Pimpernel and Heart's-ease and Corn daisy.

June 15th.   Drove to Denham Bridge in the afternoon, —
about five miles from Dousland. The bridge spans the
Tavy in a narrow wooded valley; The steep banks rising
up on either side the Combe were covered with tall
purple Fox-gloves and ferns of all varieties. Saw the first
wild Roses on a way-side hedge: Gathered Cow-wheat
and a flower of the Labiate tribe I did not-know.
(Bastard Balm)

June 16th.   Saw a Red Admiral butterfly on the moor and
found the first blossoms of the Bell-heather, also
gathered a tiny flower like Eye-bright, only deep pink in
colour, and a lovely little plant with blossoms like pink
stars lying flat on the ground.

The moor now is starred all over with the tiny
golden flowers of the Yellow Tormentil, quantities of
pink Field Louse-wort and Milk-wort of every colour.

Marsh Louse-wort.
Spotted Orchis.

Stone-crop
Fumitory

Wall Pennywort
Painted Lady Butterfl

June

June 16th. The Whin-blossom is all over; its' glory has departed till the Autumn.

June 17th. Saw a Red Admiral butterfly; picked a lot of wild Strawberries; numbers of Ghost Moths hovering over the grass in the evening now.

June 21st. Went to stay for three days at Plympton 4 miles from Plymouth; the vegetation there is much more luxuriant than on the heights of Dartmoor; The hedges were covered with wild Roses and Honey suckle, – tall grasses and Scarlet Poppies in the fields and high banks with Vetches, Bed-straws and all kinds of Umbelliferous flowers in full bloom. Gathered Frog-bit; Wild Guelder Rose, Spindle-tree blossom and Dog-wood – I noticed a great variety of Cranes-bills on the banks of the lanes.

June 24. Back to Dousland. Hay-making going on in the fields all along the line.

"*I* will forsake the cuckoo-haunted vale,
Leave the lone pastures that are all the lark's;
Stir the green depth of heather on the plain
Where the high moorland sleeps in noontide heat;
Haply to hear the stirring grouse chide me back
While aromatic fragrance wafts and fails
By pools and lakes of silver-silken grass
Shimmering responsive to the cloud-flecked blue.
Prone on the bosom of my mother earth
Thence will I lift mine eyes unto the hills,
And bitterness shall turn a heart of peace
To the broad healing of the South-west wind."

K. B.

"*The thronged boughs of the shadowy sycamore*
Still bear young leaflets half the summer through;
From where the robin 'gainst the unhidden blue
Perched dark, till now, deep in the leafy core;
The embowered throstle's urgent wood-notes soar,
Through summer silence.
Still the leaves come new;
Yet never rosy-sheathed as those which drew
Their spiral tongues from spring buds heretofore."

"THE DAY-DREAM".
D. G. ROSSETTI.

Here in the country's heart
Where the grass is green
Life is the same sweet life
As it e'er hath been

Trust in a God still lives,
And the bell at morn
Floats with a thought of God
O'er the rising corn.

God comes down in the rain
And the crop grows tall —
This is the country faith,
And the best of all!

NORMAN GALE.

June 27th.   The meadows are a perfect garden of wild flowers. Down at Huckworthy today I walked through them beside the river Walkham. The tall grass was full of Moon-daisies, Sorrel, Borage and Knap-weed, In the marshes I picked Ragged Robin and Meadow-Sweet, or Queen of the Meadow, as they call it in Scotland; there was still quantities of the Mimulus in blossom, – both the small and large varieties, and blue Forget-me-not and Water-cress.

June 28th.   Went up on the moor for the first time for a week: The purple Bell Heather is just breaking into blossom and I found patches of the pink Bog-heath or Cross-leaved Heath.

The wild Thyme and a very small species of white Bedstraw are taking the place of the Milkwort and Field Lousewort on the moor. There were numbers of Sky-larks and a few Pee-wits; the latter circling round me and crying over my head.

Bastard Balm
Common Avens.
Cow-Wheat
Fruit of Wild Strawberry
Fruit of Whortle-berry

Trailing
St. John's Wort.

Eye-brig

Upright
St. John's Wort

Devil's-bit
Scabio

"IN JUNE."

I wake with the flowers that will
    watch out the night;
    Yellow and white
In the midsummer twilight over the land
    For the dawn at hand.
From the secret and silent regions of birth
    To come on earth.
You shall find me early and leave me late
    I can always wait,
As sure as the summer and sun will disclose
    The heart of the rose,
With the brooding passion of poet or bird
    Till life be stirred
In the formless thought, in the eggs of blue,
    And love in you.
Oh, the shy delight of the rosebuds' red!
    Oh! the word unsaid!

K.B.

"*Under the Greenwood tree*
    Who loves to lie with me,
    And turn his merry note
    Unto the sweet birds' throat –
Come hither, come hither, come hither!
    Here shall he see
    No enemy
But winter and rough weather.

Who doth ambition shun
    And loves to lie i' the sun.
    Seeking the food he eats
    And pleased with what he gets –
Come hither, come hither, come hither!
    Here shall he see
    No enemy
But winter and rough weather."

W. SHAKESPEARE – 'AS YOU LIKE IT'.

Common Yellow Vetch
Tufted Purple Vetch

White Bladder Campion
Field Knautia.

Red Admiral Butterfly
Honey-suckle.

"To hear the lark begin his flight
And singing startle the dull night,
From his watch-tower in the skies
Till the dappled dawn doth rise;
Then to come, in spite of sorrow,
And at my window bid good morrow
Through the sweet-briar or the vine,
Or the twisted eglantine:
While the cock with lively din
Scatters the rear of darkness thin,
And to the stack, or the barn-door
Stoutly struts his dames before:
Oft listening how the hounds and horn
Cheerly rouse the slumbering morn,
From the side of some hoar hill
Through the high wood echoing shrill:
Sometime walking, not unseen,
By hedge-row elms, on hillocks green,
Right against the Eastern gate
Where the great Sun begins his state
Robed in flames and amber light,
The clouds in thousand liveries dight;
While the ploughman, near at hand,

June

"Whistles o'er the furrow'd land
And the milkmaid singeth blythe
And the mower whets his scythe,
And every shepherd tells his tale
Under the Hawthorn in the dale."

MILTON. 'L'ALLEGRO'.

"Give to me the life I love
Let the lave go by me;
Give the jolly heaven above,
And the highway nigh me.
Bed in the bush with stars to see;
Bread I dip in the river.
Thats' the life for a man like me
Thats' the life for ever.

"SONG". R. L. STEVENSON.

"Wreathing honey suckles winding
with the westering sun
Self entwined and twig entagled
bush and briar o'er run, –
What a mass of yellow bloom!
Clustering heads of sweet perfume!
Finger-buds of rose unfurling
Clarion trumps their tips uncurling
Opening to the azure sky
Waxen throats of minstrelsy!

"HONEYSUCKLE".
E. M. HEATH.

'Gather ye rose-buds while ye may
Old Time is still aflying
And this same flower that smiles today
Tomorrow will be dying.'
                    R. Herrick.

Wild Roses and Honeysuckle.

Cross-leaved Heath.
Bell Heather
Centory
Ivy-leaved Bell-flow

July

This month was originally the fifth of the year, and was called by the Romans Quinctilis, the latin name of Julius was given in honour of Julius Caesar, who was born in this month.

Feasts Days, etc.

July 3rd.	Dog days begin
July 5th.	St. Swithin
July 25th.	St James

"St. Swithin's Day (July 15th) if it do rain
For forty days it will remain."

"St. Swithin's Day if it be fair,
For forty days 'twill rain nae' mair."

"A swarm of bees in May is worth a load of hay,
A swarm of bees in June is worth a silver spoon,
A swarm of bees in July is not worth a fly."

"In July shear your rye".

"Blows the wind today, and the sun and the rain are flying
Blows the wind on the moor, today and now;
Where, round the graves of the martyrs the whaups all crying
My soul remembers how.

Grey, recumbent tombs of the dead, in the desert places,
Standing stones on the vacant wine-red moor,
Hills of sheep, – and the silent vanished races,
And the wind austere and pure.

Be it granted to me to behold you again in dying;
Hills of home, and to hear once more the call.
Hear round the graves of the martyrs the pee-weeps crying
And hear no more at all.

R. L. STEVENSON.

JULY

Flower of Common Bramble
Meadow Brown Butterfly.

The Lark

Waken and sing and soar—
Leaving the green earth-flo[or]
Up to the wind-swept door[s]
   The blue sky-wold;
Stained with a single st[ar]
High o'er the mountain-sca[r]
Streaked with a purple b[ar]
   Beaten with gold.

Waken and soar and sing—
Shake off the dews that cli[ng]
Spread out a fearless wing
   Cleaving the blue.
Send out a note of song
Follow the note; — and strong
Run up a scale, ere long
   Lost to the view.

Phœbus upsprings to view
Sun-God and Song-God too;
Pour forth the song anew,
   Sun-swept, song-driven,
Mount up as ne'er before,
Pour forth and still adore—
Pour forth the song, and soar
   Straight into Heaven.

Spent with a theme so vast;
Sink ere the song is past
Sink — while the music last;
   Sun-swept, song-riven;
Down to the mountain-crest
Down to the green earth-breast
Down — down — down — down;
   to rest;
   Song-spent, sun-shriven!

E. M. Holden

High o'er the mountains bare;
Hang like a speck — and the[n]
Drift in a sea of air
   Boundless as bliss;
Close to the golden gate
Where the clouds lie in sta[te]
Pause, — till the silence sate[d]
   The sun's first kiss.

Corn-cockle

July

July 1st.   Dull, cloudy day, with heavy thunder showers.

July 3rd.   Gathered Rest-harrow, Blackberry blossom, Knap-weed, (two species) and pink Centory. There are two distinct kinds of Blackberry blossom growing here, One with very large pink blossoms with five petals, the other white, with double the number of petals. The strawberries are very plentiful now on all the banks. Heard the Night-jar.

July 6th.   Walked across the moors to Nun's Cross, and back by Leather Tor. Gloriously bright day with very clear, distant views. Saw some dark blue Dragon-flies by one of the little streams trickling through the bog; and Fritillary Butterflies. Great stretches of heather, but only small patches of the Bell Heather and pink Bog-heath in blossom as yet.

July

July 9th.   Gathered Corn-flower and a tiny purple Campanula growing beside the Leat. Heard the shrill notes of the night-jar at half past nine in the evening through an open window, Went out and watched a pair chasing each other through the air; but they did not alight on the ground, and their flight was so swift I could not see them clearly.

July 11th.   Going along Meavy Lane I saw a thrush with a snail in its' beak; I watched it carry it to a big stone in the middle of the road and dash it several times against the stone before it picked it out of the shell to eat it.

July 13th.   Went to Princetown by train and walked from there to Dartmeet and back across the moors to Dousland – about twelve miles: The heather is still very little out. On an old bridge over the Dart I saw some Golden Rod in blossom.

Bog Asphodel.
Bog Pimpernel.
Wild Thyme.

Sundew
Mush-rooms.
Common Adder or Viper

Wren's nest
in wall.

Rocks on Vixen Tor.

Dartmoor Pony & foal.

July 15th.   Gathered some pure white Heath on Yannadon Down, – of both species, – the Cross-leaved Heath and the purple Bell-heather. Bog Pimpernel and Bog Asphodel in blossom in the marshes on the banks of Burrator; Saw a stoat coming up Lowry Lane, it ran up the hill between the walls for a quite a long way in front of me. A bed of nettles I passed today was quite black with the caterpillars of the Pea-cock Butterfly.

July 17th.   Went to the top of Peak Hill to sketch, Some wild pigeons who flew down among the rocks and a pair of Missel Thrushes and Crows were the only living things I saw up there. Sheep and ponies and cows were visible in the distance, feeding on the slopes of Leather Tor.

The rocks on the tors are thick with Bilberry bushes, covered now with fruit.

July 18th.   Going through the fields to Walkhampton I have constantly noticed a little wren fly out from a certain place in the wall; I thought it was seeking for insects in the crannies between the stones, but today I discovered a nest made of dried grasses, with a number of eggs. This is the latest in the season I have ever found.

July 19th.   Gathered a number of Mush-rooms; A Viper was brought in, killed near Vixen Tor today.

July 22nd.   Walked to Drizzle Combe and Ditsworthy Warren to see the stone-rows and Menhirs. Gathered White Heath of both species and Sundew just coming into blossom. Saw hundreds of rabbits at Ditsworthy. In some places the moor was riddled with their holes. In one part of the moor there was a great stretch of pink Bog-heath, about an acre in extent; it made a beautiful patch of colour; Here and there some pure white blossoms shone out very distinctly among the pink.

Common Cotton Thistle
and Wild Bees.

Greater Knapweed
Discoid Knapweed.

July 22nd. On the way home I saw a dead Grass Snake about two feet long hanging on a bough.

July 26th. Walked to Vixen Tor, past Samford Spiney, and the valley of the Walkham river. Saw numbers of beautiful Fritillary butterflies. On the lower slopes of the Tor were thickets of Hazel-nut bushes covered with fruit and twined all about with Honey-suckle creeper full of blossom – very white and large.

July 27th. Found some of the little white blossom of the Dodder; the curious little parasite that grows on the heather.

August

August received its' name from the Emperor Augustus. He was not born in August, but during this month his greatest good fortune happened to him: As July contained thirty one days and August only thirty; it was thought necessary to add another day to the latter month, in order that Augustus might not be in any respect inferior to Julius.

"All the tears St. Swithin can cry
St. Bartholemy's mantle wipes them dry".

"St Bartholomew (August 24th)
Brings the cold dew."

"If the 24th of August be fair and clear
Then hope for a prosperous Autumn that year".

Dock
Hawkweed
Common Blue Butterfly

August

Dodder

Common Ling

Green Grasshopper

Away o'er the brow of the hill that is
  purple with heather;
Where the pasturing bees hum alone
  thro' the long summer day.
Where the lichen-clad boulders sleep
  on thro' the centuries' weather
And the sheperding winds pipe the
  tenderest midsummer lay
As they call up the clouds from
  magnificent dreaming together;
There floats down the valley a voice
  that is fresh as the May.

From 'Bell Heather'
E.M. Holden.

DARTSIDE

I cannot tell what you say, green leaves,
  I cannot tell what you say:
But I know that there is a spirit in you,
  And a word in you this day.

I cannot tell what you say, brown streams,
  I cannot tell what you say;
But I know that in you too a spirit doth live,
  And a word doth speak this day.

'Oh green is the colour of faith and truth,
  And rose the colour of love and youth
  And brown of the fruitful day.
Sweet Earth is faithful and fruitful and young,
And her bridal day shall come ere long,
And you shall know what the rivers and the streams
And the whispering woodlands say.'

C. KINGSLEY

Drew's Teignton. Dartmoor,
July 31. 1849.

127

Aug. 1.   Bright, breezy day.

3rd.   Three species of Thistle in bloom. Wasps plentiful.

5th.   Goat's Beard and large purple Scabious looking beautiful now among the barley and oats.

8th.   Corn-cutting going on in the fields.

12th.   Gorse coming into blossom again on the moors; making bits of the moor look gorgeous, gold among the deep crimson Bell Heather and the Ling.

15th.   Gathered some white Ling and Bell Heather on Yannadon Down. Saw a small brown Lizard with a part of its' half cast skin still sticking to its' back. Saw a Painted Lady butterfly; – the third this week; and two Pea-cock butter-flies.

18th.   Blackberries beginning to ripen and Rowan berries turning scarlet.

Thrush
and
Rowan berries.

Fruit of Common Bramble.

Aug. 29.   Eclipse of the sun, commencing 11.45.a.m. lasting until 2.10.p.m. Very clear view of it.

31st.   Went up on the moor to sketch, saw several Peacock and Red Admiral butterflies as well as small Blues. The Heath is getting over now, but the Ling is just in its' prime.

One lesson, Nature, let me learn of thee,
One lesson, that in every wind is blown
One lesson of two duties serv'd in one
Though the loud world proclaim their enmity –
Of Toil unsevered from Tranquillity,
Of Labour that in still advance outgrows
Far noisier schemes, accomplished in Repose,
Too great for haste, too high for rivalry.
Yes; while on earth a thousand discords ring,
Man's senseless uproar mingling with his toil,
Still do thy sleepless ministers move on,
Their glorious tasks in silence perfecting:
Still working, blaming still our vain turmoil
Labourers that shall not fail, when man is gone.

MATTHEW ARNOLD.

September

September, – the seventh month of the old Roman year. By the Julian arrangement, it became the ninth month but still retained its' former name.

Feast Days.

Sept. 8th.   Nativity of the Blessed Virgin.
Sept 14th.   The Exaltation of the Holy Cross
Sept 21st.   St. Matthew the Apostle
Sept 29th.   St Michael the Archangel; (Michaelmas.)

"Plant trees at Michaelmas & command them to grow;
Set them at Candlemas & entreat them to grow

"Go – bring me poppies! – airy forms and slight,
Tethered to earth and drunk with sun and wind;
Gathered from gardens sown for sweet Delight,
Or graves where Ruin sits, with ampler mind.

Bring scarlet blisses blown from Ceres' heart
In young green cornfields wantonly o'er-run,
With hairy buds, whose separate sheathes dispart
O'er pensive banners, creased and silken-spun.

Bring large white globes that light the world of sleep
And yellow moons from some lone waste of sand
And set returning sail, and skim the deep
With such as grow in that far southern land:–

POPPIES. E. M. HOLDEN.

September

Menhirs & Stone-rows at Drizzle-combe

View across the Meavy Valley
from Yannadon Down.

September

"Go, for they call you, Shepherd, from the hill;
    Go, Shepherd, and untie the wattled cotes;
    No longer leave the wistful flock unfed,
Nor let thy bawling fellows rack their throats,
    Nor the cropp'd grasses shoot another head.
    But when the fields are still,
And the tired men and dogs all gone to rest,
    And only the white sheep are sometimes seen
    Cross and recross the strips of moon-blanch'd green;
Come, Shepherd, and again renew the quest.

Here, where the reaper was at work of late,
    In this high field's dark corner, where he leaves
    His coat, his basket, and his earthen cruise,
And in the sun all morning finds the sheaves
    Then here, at noon, comes back his store to use;
    Here will I sit and wait.
While to my ear from uplands far away
    The bleating of the folded flocks is borne;
    With distant cries of reapers in the corn. –
All the live murmur of a summer's day."

'THE SCHOLAR GYPSY'. MATTHEW ARNOLD

Sept. 1st.   Showery day, with cold northwest breezes

Sept. 5th.   Walked to Vixen Tor; fine stretches of dwarf gorse in bloom

Sept 8th.   Drove to Tavy Cleave, through Tavistock and Mary Tavy, quantities of Blackberries in the hedges. The slopes of the tors on either side the Tavy covered with gorse and heather in blossom

Sept. 12th.   Drove to Dartmeet from Prince-town. Gorgeous colouring everywhere. Parts of the high lying moorland are white with short bleached grasses contrasting strongly with the dark patches of purple heather and gold of the gorse. The valley below the meeting of the East and West Darts was a perfect picture

Sept. 18th.   Left Dartmoor with great regret and travelled back to Olton.

Sept. 22nd.   The hedges are full of berries now, Hips and Haws; Elder-berries and Black-berries are the most conspicious, also the bright crimson berries of the Bitter-sweet. There is a plentiful crop of Acorns and Chesnuts.

Sept. 23rd.   Found some curious galls on the leaves of the Willow bushes growing round Alton Mill-pool, – making the trees look as if they were covered with green and red berries.

Sept. 24th.   There are some fine trees of the Horse Chesnut on Olton Golf-course, covered with fruit, and one or two of the Spanish or Sweet Chesnut, one mass of prickly balls. I gathered some today from the low-hanging boughs and brought them home to paint

Sept. 25.   Cycled to Knowle through Widney, I saw some of the white blooms of the Greater Bindweed and sprays of Honey-suckle in blossom in several places in the hedges.

September

"*Season of mists and mellow fruitfulness!*
Close bosom-friend of the maturing sun;
Conspiring with him how to load and bless
With fruits the vines that round the thatch-eaves run;
To bend with apples the moss'd cottage trees,
And fill all fruits with ripeness to the core;
To swell the gourd, and plump the hazel shells
With a sweet kernel; to set budding more,
And still more, later flowers for the bees,
Until they think warm days will never cease,
For Summer has o'er brimm'd their clammy cells.

J KEATS:- "TO AUTUMN".

Calm and deep peace on this high wold,
And on these dews that drench the furze,
And all the silvery gossamers
That twinkle into green and gold.

Calm and still light on yon great plain
That sweeps with all its' Autumn bowers,
And crowded farms and lessening towers,
To mingle with the bounding main."

TENNYSON – "IN MEMORY".

138

Fruit
of Horse-Chesnut.

Fruit
of
Sweet Chesnut

Sept. 25th.   Gathered some of the crimson berries of the wild Guelder-rose and the Wild Service-tree. The Chesnut and Poplar trees are all turning yellow and the Blackberry leaves are all shades of crimson and gold now.

Sept. 28th.   Wandered along to the Golf-course this morning there are very few wild flowers left in bloom now; – a few Corn-daisies and a kind of Hawk-weed, with some belated Blackberry blossoms were the only ones I saw. Further out in the country there would doubtless be many more.

September

"Behold her, single in the field
Yon solitary Highland Lass!
Reaping and singing by herself;
Stop here, or gently pass!
Alone she cuts and binds the grain
And sings a melancholy strain;
O listen! for the Vale profound
Is overflowing with the sound.

No nightingale did ever chaunt
More welcome notes to weary hands
Of travellers in some shady haunt
Among Arabian sands:
A voice so thrilling ne'er was heard
In spring-time from the cuckoo-bird
Breaking the silence of the seas
Among the farthest Hebrides.

Will no-one tell me what she sings?
Perhaps the plaintive numbers flow
For old, unhappy, far-off things,
And battles long ago:
Or is it some more humble lay,
Familiar matter of today?
Some natural sorrow, loss or pain,
That has been, and may be again?

Whate'er the theme, the Maiden sang
As if her song could have no ending
I saw her singing at her work
And o'er the sickle bending; –
I listened, motionless and still;
And as I mounted up the hill,
The music in my heart I bore
Long after it was heard no more."

'THE SOLITARY REAPER'.
W. WORDSWORTH.

142

Greater Bindweed
and
Wild. Guelder Rose berries.

Fruit of
Hawthorne
and
Wild Service Tree.

September

AUTUMN

"With what a glory goes and comes the year!
The buds of spring, those beautiful harbingers
Of sunny skies and cloudless times, enjoy
Life's newness, and earth's garniture spread out;
And when the silver habit of the clouds
Comes down upon the Autumn sun, and with
A sober gladness the old year takes up
His bright inheritance of golden fruits,
A pomp and pageant fill the splendid scene.

There is a beautiful spirit breathing now.
Its' mellow richness on the clustered trees,
And from a beaker full of richest dyes,
Pouring new glory on the Autumn woods,
And dipping in warm light the pillared clouds
Morn on the mountain, like a summer bird,
Lifts up her purple wing, and in the vales
The gentle Wind, a sweet and passionate wooer,
Kisses the blushing leaf, and stirs up life
Within the solemn woods of ash deep-crimsoned

And silver beech, and maple yellow-leaved,
Where Autumn, like a faint old man, sits down
By the wayside aweary. Through the trees
The golden robin moves. The purple finch
That on wild cherry and red cedar gives
A winter bird, comes with its' plaintive whistle,
And pecks by the witch-hazel, whilst aloud
From cottage-roofs the warbling blue-bird sings;
And merrily with oft-repeated stroke,
Sounds from the threshing-floor the busy flail.

Oh, what a glory does this world put on
For him, who with a fervent heart, goes forth
Under the bright and glorious sky and looks
On duties well performed and days well spent.
For him the wind, ay and the yellow leaves,
Shall have a voice, and give him eloquent teachings
He shall so hear the solemn hymn that Death
Has lifted up for all, that he shall go
To his long resting-place without a tear."

LONGFELLOW

145

October

This was the eighth month of the old Roman year. By the Slavs this month is called "yellow month" from the fading of the leaf. To the Anglo Saxons it was known as "Winter fylleth", because at this full moon (Fylleth) winter was supposed to begin.

Saints' Days etc.

Oct. 18th.   St. Luke.
Oct. 28.   St. Simon and St. Jude.
Oct. 31st.   Hallowe'en.

"By the 1st of March the crows begin to search
By the 1st of april they are sitting still
By the 1st of May they are flown away
Creeping greedy back again
With October wind and rain.

"A good October and a good blast
To blow the hog, acorn and mast."

October

Berries of the Bittersweet
and
Elderberry tree.

Oct. 1st.   Cold, showery day.

Oct 2nd.   Walked along the Elmdon road; I noticed that nearly all the Elderberries had been stripped from the bushes; these and the Rowans are the first Autumn berries the birds choose. Saw a Kingfisher skimming across a pond by the roadside, it made a glowing picture, with its' emerald plumage against the dark brown water and the overhanging boughs of a maple tree all gold and red. I saw one Sycamore tree quite leafless; but a great many of the trees are still green.

Oct. 3rd   Strong westerly gale; The leaves coming down in showers from the trees.

Oct. 6th.   There is a fine harvest of Beech-mast this year, the ground beneath the trees is strewn with empty shells and ripe kernals and there are still plenty to fall. The foliage of the Beech tree is just beginning to turn its' rich golden red, the Horse-chesnuts have long since put on their Autumn glory of gold.

"*A spirit haunts the year's last hours*
Dwelling amid these yellowing bowers:
      To himself he talks;
For at eventide, listening earnestly;
At his work you may hear him sob and sigh
      In the walks;
Earthward he boweth the heavy stalks
Of the mouldering flowers;
      Heavily hangs the broad sunflower
      Over its' grave i' the earth so chilly;
      Heavily hangs the hollyhock
      Heavily hangs the tiger-lily.

The air is damp, and hushed, and close,
As a sick man's room when he taketh repose
      An hour before death;
My very heart faints and my whole soul grieves
At the moist, rich smell of the rotting leaves.
      And the breath
      Of the fading edges of box beneath
      And the year's last rose.
      Heavily hangs the broad sunflower
      Over its' grave in' the earth so chilly
      Heavily hangs the holly hock,
      Heavily hangs the tiger-lily."
                                             'SONG'. TENNYSON.

Squirrel and
Beechmast

Hazel-nuts
and
Acorns

Oct. 6th. I have been out to search for Sloes; The bushes were covered with blossom in the spring, but I cannot find a trace of fruit anywhere. I visited a hedge of Wild Bullace that was a mass of white blossom last May, but not a berry could I find; Is this due to the late frosts we had in May, that prevented the fruit setting?

Oct. 9th. Cycled over to Baddesley Clinton. I was surprised to see how green the trees still are; but the hedges were everywhere splendid with the berries and foliage of the Wild Rose, Hawthorn, Small Maple and Crab-apple.

Oct 11th. Saw a pair of Gold-finches feeding on a piece of waste land beside the canal close to Olton station.

Oct. 12th. Walked to Elmdon Park through the fields. I came upon a small Crab-apple tree in the hedge laden with apples, I tried to gather some on the bough, but all the apples fell to the ground, directly I grasped the branch.

Oct 12th. Fungi of all kinds are plentiful now, I noticed some Champignon mushrooms of great size in one field, and a very pretty fungus; bright red above and orange beneath. The cows were standing knee-deep in the pool where I saw the kingfisher a fortnight ago; the Beech-trees have turned very much since then, and some of the Elms that were green, are now quite yellow. There are three Wild Service trees growing on the bank of a pool at the edge of the park, they are all covered with fruit; and the largest of the three, overhanging the path is a perfect blaze of crimson; There were droves of Pheasants in all the stubble and clover fields; they were quite tame and only moved a little farther away from the pathway on my approach, I saw several coveys of partridges too.

Greenfinches
and
Wild Rose·berries.

Crab-Apples
Wild Sloe and Bullace.

'By the rose-flesh mushrooms—undivulged
last evening—Nay, in today's first dew
Yon sudden coral nipple bulged,
Where a freak'd, fawn-coloured, flaky crew
Of toad-stools peep indulged'.

R. Browning

Oct. 12.   There is some fine timber in the park itself, a grove of Birch trees looked lovely – the tiny leaves on the pendant branches looked like showers of gold. The rabbits were scurrying about everywhere; and I saw flocks of Thrushes and finches busy with the Hawthorn berries; I heard a Woodpecker laughing somewhere among the trees. The birds are beginning to sing again now; I heard several Robins on my way. I discovered two Sloe-berries on a bush and brought them home in triumph. The Knapweed and pink Campion are still in bloom, the latter very small and pale and I noticed a great many blossoms of the Procumbent Speedwell in one field.

October

"Autumn Clouds are flying, flying
　　O'er the waste of blue;
Summer flowers are dying, dying
　　Late so lovely new
Labouring wains are slowly rolling
　　Home with laden grain;
Holy bells are slowly tolling
　　Over buried men.

Goldener lights set noon asleeping
　　Like an afternoon;
Colder airs come stealing, creeping
　　After sun and moon;
And the leaves, all tired of blowing
　　Cloudlike o'er the sun;
Change to sunset colours, knowing
　　That their day is done.

Autumn's sun is sinking, pinking
　　Into Winter's night;
And our hearts are thinking, thinking
　　Of the cold and flight.
Our life's sun is slowly going
　　Down the hill of might.
Will our clouds shine golden-glowing
　　On the slope of night?

But the vanished corn is lying
　　In rich golden glooms.
In the churchyard, all the sighing
　　Is above the tombs.
Spring will come, slow-lingering
　　Opening buds of faith;
Man goes forth to meet his spring
　　Through the door of death."

GEORGE MACDONALD.

October tints.

Young Catkins
on Alder and Hazel-nut.

October

Oct. 19th.   Bright, frosty morning. Walked through the fields to get some leaves and berries. The birds were busy everywhere among the berries in the hedges; there were a great many Blackbirds and thrushes and I noticed a Redwing among the latter, the first I have seen this Autumn. The trees with their Autumn colouring looked very beautiful in the bright sunshine, one Elm tree was specially lovely, the foliage on the lower boughs was pale green, a little higher up pale yellow; deepening in colour all the way up, till at the top it was deep gold.

The frost seems to have spoiled the pretty, bright fungi; they were lying all about the field, shrunken and discoloured; but there were a good many brown ones that seem to be of a hardier kind.

I saw a tiny Golden-crested Wren creeping about the lower boughs of a Spanish Chesnut. It did not seem at all alarmed at my approach, but allowed me to go quite close up and watch it in its' hunt after insects.

October

Oct. 19th.   The little new Catkins are appearing on the Hazel-nut bushes and the Alder-trees.

„ 27th.   Saw a Heron at the edge of the reservoir.

Oct. 29th.   Saw a King-fisher flying along the Canal-bank at Olton.

Oct. 31st.   Halloweven or Hallow'een, the vigil of Hallowmas or All Saints' Day.

"Thought to be a night when witches, devils, and other mischief-making beings are all abroad on their baneful, midnight errands; particularly those aerial people, the fairies are said on that night to hold a grand anniversary."   ETTRICK SHEPHERD.

"*Upon that night, when fairies light,*
On Cassilis Downans dance,
Or owre the lays, in splendid blaze
On sprightly coursers prance;
Or for Colian the route is ta'en,
Beneath the moon's pale beams;
There up the cove to stray and rove
Amang the rocks and streams,
To sport that night."   BURNS. "HALLOWEEN".

November

Seed vessels

November

November was the ninth month of the old Roman year. The 11th of November was held to mark the beginning of winter. The Anglo Saxon name of November was Blotmonath (blood month) probably alluding to the slaughter of cattle for winter consumption.

Principal feast-days in the Roman calendar

Nov. 1st.	All Saints' Day
„ 2nd.	All Souls' Day
3rd.	St Hubert.
11th.	St. Martin's
21st.	Presentation of the Virgin.
22nd.	St. Cecilia
25th.	St Catherine
30th.	St Andrew

In the English Calender, All Saints and St. Andrew's are the only feasts retained.

Nov. 5th.   Bonfire Night. The particular service commemorative of the Papists' conspiracy on the 5th. was abolished in 1859.

November

"November take flail
Let no ships sail."

"If there's ice in November that will bear a duck
There'll be nothing after but sludge and muck."

"Please to remember the fifth of November,
Gun-powder treason and plot;
I see no reason why gun-powder treason
Should ever be forgot."

Soft as the bloom on the cheeks of the morning
Frail as the foam on a wind-driven sea;
Faint as a sail in the dim distance dawning,
Like to a fairy flotilla set free, –
Floats the white thistle down over the lea,
Sails the silk thistle down out to the sea,
Filling the air like a phantom of glee.

Here is a chain of the æronauts sailing
Close to the downs in a voyage of ease
There goes a shuttle cock wantonly scaling
Heaven itself in a sport of the breeze
Others – they tarry, – the range not, – and these
Who but a flock of grey linnets shall seize,
Little grey linnets in twos and in threes?

FROM "THISTLEDOWN" BY E. M. HOLDEN.

Linnet
and
Thistle-seed.

Nov. 1.   Wet, chilly day. Troops of Starlings and Sparrows come to feed

3rd.   every morning on the lawn now.

4th.   Thick fog in the morning, Cycled to Knowle. There were thousands of tiny cobwebs sparkling with dew-drops all along the hedge-rows.

5th.   This morning when I opened my window there was quite a chorus of birds' voices. A Blackbird and Thrush were singing and I heard a Robin's voice and the Starling were twittering away most energetically up among the eaves.

7th.   Yesterday I erected a short pole in the garden with a small, flat board on the top, to serve as a breakfast table for the birds; I strewed it with crumbs and bits of meat; but all day yesterday the birds left it severely alone. This morning a Starling summoned up courage to alight on it; the Sparrows followed and by and bye came two Tom-tits. After that there was a constant succession of visitors all through the day. Blue-tits, Great-tits and Robins as well as Starlings & Sparrows.

"*M*ourner, who wanderest gray and mute
O'er mouldering leaves and fallen fruit
    Weep unreproved!
Thou art not for thy sombre suit
    The less beloved.

Welcome as April's bridal tears
Or the ripe smile September wears
    Are thy grave eyes
Made wistful with the agèd years'
    Dim memories.

Thine are the dawns of solemn sheen
Through interwoven branches seen
    As when doth smile
Through some cathedral's carven screen
    The Alters' light.

Thou lendest darkness to the yew
The distant hills a deeper blue
    Thy footsteps wake
Mosses to flower, when flowers are few
    In leafless brake.

November

The mellow year is hastening to its close;
The little birds have almost sung their last,
Their small notes twitter in the dreary blast—
That shrill-piped harbinger of early snows;
The patient beauty of the scentless rose,
Oft with the morn's hoar crystal quaintly glassed;
Hangs a pale mourner for the summer past,
And makes a little summer where it grows:
In the chill sunbeam of the faint brief day
The dusky waters shudder as they shine;
The russet leaves obstruct the straggling way
Of oozy brooks, which no deep banks define,
And the gaunt woods, in ragged scant array
Wrap their old limbs with sombre ivy-twine.

Hartley Coleridge

Dock-See

November

Fair as the liveliest summer dress
The beeche's silver nakedness
    When red and gold
That robed her for the storm's caress
    Her feet enfold.

Through steel blue clouds a gleaming wedge
Strikes on the berry-jewelled hedge
    And dusky wood
On osiers smooth and tawny sedge
    And streams in flood.

And as a child's light laugh beguiles
Sorrow to lose herself in smiles;
    The red-breasts' lay
Maketh the woodland's silent aisles
    Seem almost gay.

Tis good to watch the loose clouds driven
When the broad south their web hath riven,
    or pace again
Beneath a calm, snow-burdened heaven
    The darkening lane.

November

Strewn with the maple's moth-like seeds
And catch the scent of smouldering weeds
　　O'er brown waves borne
Of fresh-ploughed warm and silent meads
　　And corn-fields shorn.

Tis good to feel thy tear-drops fall
Upon the dead fern's quiet pall
　　Of purple mist.
When frost for their snow-burial
　　The wolds hath kissed.

But best to watch – when deathlike eve
The pensive landscape doth bereave
　　Of short-lived day –
Thy great pathetic sunsets grieve
　　Their hearts away.

ALFRED HAYES.

December

In the Roman calandar, the year was divided into ten months; the last of which was called December or the tenth months; and this name was retained for the last or twelfth month of the year as now divided. The Saxons called it 'Winter-monat' or Winter month, and "Heligh-monat", – Holy month, from the fact that Christmas falls within it. The 22nd of December is the date of the winter solstice, when the sun reaches the tropic of Capricorn.

Saints' Days etc.

Dec. 24.	Christmas Eve
Dec. 25.	Christmas Day.
Dec. 27.	St. Thomas' Day
Dec. 31st.	New Year's Day.

Mottoes: *"In December keep yourself warm and sleep."*

"Bounce Buckram velvets' dear,
Christmas comes but once a year,
When it comes it brings good cheer,
When it's gone it's never near."

December

In rigorous hours, when down the iron lane
The redbreast looks in vain
For hips and haws,
Lo; shining flowers upon my window-pane
The silver pencil of the winter draws.

When all the snowy hill
And the bare woods are still
When snipes are silent in the frozen bogs
And all the garden garth is whelmed in mire,
Lo, by the hearth, the laughter of the logs —
More fair than roses, lo, the flowers of fire!

'WINTER'. R. L. STEVENSON

"That time of year thou may'st in me behold
When yellow leaves, or none, or few, do hang
Upon those boughs, which shake against the cold
Bare, ruined choirs, where late the sweet birds sang."

SONNET. SHAKESPEARE.

December

Blackbird
Robin
Hedge-sparrows
Blue-tit.
Ivy and Holly

Cole Tits.

Blue Tits

Dec. 3.   Since I hung the cocoa-nut up to the ledge of the birds breakfast-table a few days ago, the Tom-tits have been much more numerous. Hardly an hour of the day, but one or more of them is to be seen, working away inside the shell.

Dec. 7th.   I have been counting how many different kinds of birds come to be fed every morning. So far I have counted nine. Sparrows of course are far more numerous than any other variety; then come Starlings, then Tom-tits – three varieties, – Great Tits, Blue Tits and Cole Tits, then Hedge-sparrows, Robins, Blackbirds and Thrushes. I have seen a big black Rook hovering about once or twice, but he has never summoned up courage to alight so near the house.

Dec. 18th.   The weather up till now has been very mild and open, we have had only one slight snow-shower this winter and only one spell of severe frost.

December

"*Heap on more wood! – the wind is chill,*
But let it whistle as it will,
We'll keep our Christmas merry still;
'Twas Christmas broached the mightiest ale;
'Twas Christmas told the merriest tale;
A Christmas gambol oft could cheer
The poor man's heart through half the year."

SIR WALTER SCOTT.

"*Some say that ever 'gainst that season comes*
Wherein our Saviours' birth is celebrated,
The bird of dawning singeth all night long,
And then, they say, no spirit dares stir abroad;
The nights are wholesome, then no planets strike
No fairy takes, nor witch hath power to charm
So hallow'd and so gracious is the time."

SHAKESPEARE.

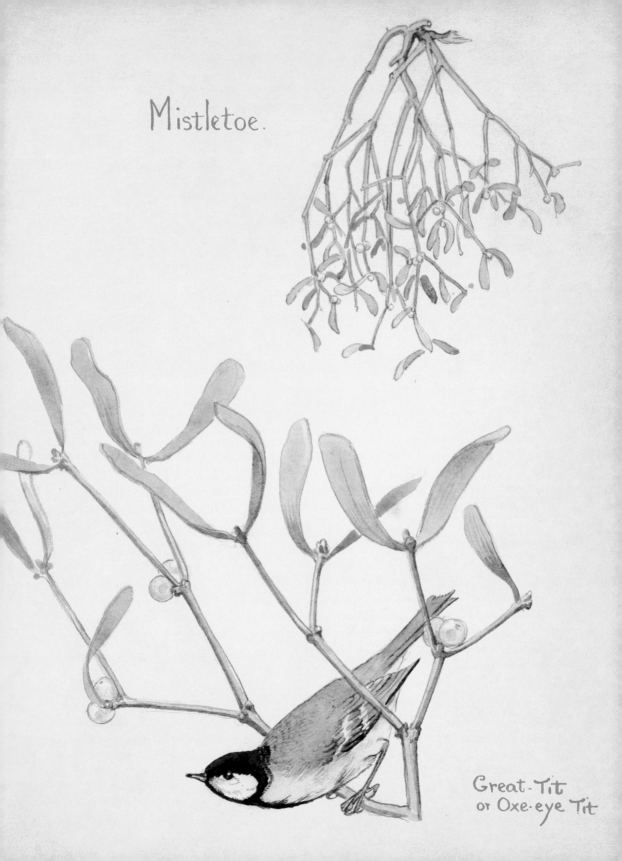

Mistletoe.

Great-Tit
or Oxe-eye Tit

The Robin

I love the lark that cleaves the morning skie
And that inspired recluse the nightingale
I love the wandering voice that cuckoo cries
And doves that plead anon in beechen val

I love the throstle whistling in the rain,
And golden-bill a-carol on the thorn;
And many a treble pipe and lilting strain
That comes with spring and revels in the da

But oh, when all the red and russet fires
Have waned at last along the woodland way
How fresh and clear amid the ruined choirs
The wild, sweet snatches of the robin's lay

Trim-suited bard!—beneath that ruddy vest
The lyric soul of music surely lives.
And as it takes with storm his tiny breast
He little knows the joy to me he gives;

But hops away amid the matted leaves
His beady eyes as black as shining jet,
While still with tears the stricken forest gri
Whose every bough is hung with jewels wet.

He is the friend of yon secluded cot.
And when the wood is wreathed in wintry sno
Full many a crumb from no unstinted lar
The labourer's wife to Robin Redbreast throw

And though mid hardy frost he scarce may sing
When surly fiends the very streams congeal
And o'er the wold, the storm on scudding wing
Bids every lesser bird himself conceal.

Yet soon once more from some sequestered nook
Of rambling barn or overhanging reef,
Or ivied bank beside the running brook
He drops as lightly as a withered leaf.

And sings again the song we ne'er despise
Yet scarce remember mid o'erwhelming fate, —
Of secret Joy — that never wholly dies
Nor is less sweet because the spring is late.

Until methinks there lurks within his breast
A merry elf that babbles of the hour
When first the forest in its splendour dressed
Becomes the paradise of bird and flower.

And through the silvery dusk of woodland ways
The piping spring with all her feathered train
And tripping elves and laughing flowers and fays
Returns, — like sunshine after snow and rain.

E.M.H.

Dec. 25th. – Christmas Day. Mild and spring-like. Three Primroses in bloom in the garden.

Dec. 29th. Two rainy days in succession, the first we have had for many weeks.

Dec. 31st. Bitter east wind and black frost. Walked to Elmdon park; On the way saw a large fox, quite grey in colour trotting across a field. He stood to have a long gaze at us and then promptly disappeared into a wood at the edge of the field.
Berried Holly very plentiful this winter.

"Tonight the winds begin to rise
And roar from yonder dripping day
The last red leaf is whirled away
The Rooks are blown about the skies."

TENNYSON.

December

"When icicles hang by the wall
And Dick the shepherd blows his nail
And Tom bears logs into the hall
And milk comes frozen home in pail
When blood is nipped and ways be foul,
Then nightly sings the staring owl,
      To-whit!
    To-who! – a merry note;
While greasy Joan doth keel the pot.

When all aloud the wind doth blow
And coughing drowns the parson's saw,
And birds sit brooding in the snow,
And Marian's nose looks red and raw.
When roasted crabs hiss in the bowl
Then nightly sings the staring owl,
      To-whit!
    To-who! – a merry note,
While greasy Joan doth keel the pot."

SHAKESPEARE.

White
or
Barn·Owl.

When cats run home and light is come
And dew is cold upon the ground
And the far-off stream is dumb;
And the whirring sail goes round;
And the whirring sail goes round;
    Alone and warming his five wits.
    The white owl in the belfry sits.

When merry milkmaids click the latch
And rarely smells the new-mown hay
And the cock hath sung beneath the thatch
Twice or thrice his roundelay
Twice or thrice his roundelay
    Alone and warming his five wits,
    The white owl in the belfry sits.
            The Owl – Tennyson

Holly

Common Ivy

December

"So now is come our joyful'st feast
Let every man be jolly;
Each room with ivy leaves is drest
And every post with holly.
And while thus inspired we sing,
Let all the streets with echoes ring
Woods and hills and everything
Bear witness we are merry."

GEO. WITHER.

The Mistletoe (*Viscum album*) is one of a family of parasites. In England it is most abundant on the Apple-tree, more rarely on the Oak. The berries are eaten by most birds, particularly by the Missel-thrush, to which it gives its' name. It is through the agency of the birds that the plant is propagated; the viscous nature of the fruit causes it to adhere to the birds' beak, and in the bird's efforts to rid itself of the sticky substance by wiping its' beak against a tree, the seeds are transferred to the bark. The Druids held the Mistletoe in great reverence. Pliny says they esteemed it as a gift sent from heaven and held the tree on which it was found as sacred. He says too they called it "All-heal."

"Full knee-deep lies the winter snow
And the winter winds are wearily sighing
Toll ye the church-bell sad and slow,
And tread softly and speak low
For the old year lies a-dying.

　Old year you must not die
　You came to us so readily
　You lived with us so steadily
　Old year you shall not die.

He was full of joke and jest
But his merry quips are o'er
To see him die, across the waste
His son and heir doth ride post-haste
But he'll be dead before.

　Everyone for his own
　The night is starry and cold, my friend
　And the new-year, blithe and bold, my friend
　Comes up to take his own.

His face is growing sharp and thin
Alack! Our friend is gone;
Close up his eyes, tie up his chin,
Step from the corpse and let him in
That standeth there alone.

　And waiteth at the door.
　There's a new foot on the floor, my friend
　And a new face at the door, my friend
　A new face at the door.

'THE DEATH OF THE OLD YEAR'. TENNYSON.

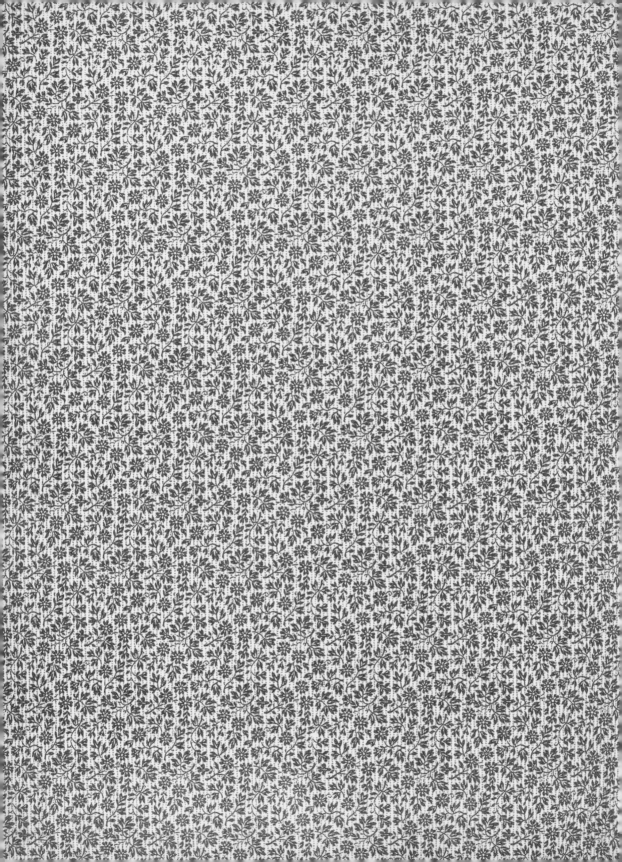